Guatemala

In Pictures

Keith Hern

Jany 2021
12-13 Antigua
15-17 Atitlan
17 Guatemala City

First published in 2011

© Copyright 2011

Keith Hern

Paperback ISBN13 978-1-908218-00-1

eBook ISBN 978-1-908218-02-5

Mobipocket/Kindle ISBN 978-1-908218-01-8

Published in the UK by MX Publishing,

335, Princess Park Manor, Royal Drive, London, N11 3GX

www.mxpublishing.com

Cover by www.staunch.com

Introduction

During a previous visit to Central America in the 1990s the people we stayed with were extolling the virtues of what a beautiful place Guatemala is to visit. That recommendation has stayed with me ever since, and in December 2010 I finally took the opportunity to go and have a look for myself.

Also, in the back of my mind, my wife and I are planning to take a year out and travel overland from the top of Canada to the foot of Chile continuing round into Argentina and Uruguay. Some further research into Central America would never be wasted, quite apart from the anticipation of visiting another new country.

The itinerary selected was chosen to ensure the opportunity was there to cover as wide a selection of the country as possible given the short duration of the visit. A mixture of historical Mayan ruins in the rain forest, volcano-surrounded lakes, and colourful towns with cobblestone streets made for a varied and fascinating insight into the country. As ever, the true colour is only really provided by the people and their traditions. Based on what I saw it would be fantastic to return and spend a little longer seeing some more of this stunning country.

This is my second photographic book and will certainly not be the last as it's a great way to share the sights of different countries in this colourful world. If you would like to find out more about my photography please visit my website www.keithhern.com , or follow my blog at www.keithhern.wordpress.com . If there are any questions or comments please drop me a line to: keith@keithhern.com.

Dedication

This book is dedicated to all those who have supported me in my photographic career to date, and helped make this possible – many, many thanks.

Early morning view from Avenida Norte, with Agua Volcano in the background, Antigua.

Warming early sunlight along a side street, Antigua.

Brightly coloured houses, a common site in Antigua.

'Owned' by the National Hospital, or should that be 'previously owned'?

Colourful contrast on an Antiguan side street.

Friendly newsagent on the corner of Central Park.

Stylish frontage of the Municipal Offices, Antigua.

Entrance to The Santiago Museum (Old Weapons), Antigua.

Most popular form of Antiguan transport under the watchful eyes of the police.

Typically colourful street scene in Antigua.

Father & son street musicians close to the municipal market.

Looking back up Avenida Nord to the Santa Catalina arch.

One of many busy alleyways into the crowded and lively municipal market.

Fire officer fundraising on the edge of market, Antigua.

Getting involved with the local kids' games by the municipal market.

Impressively colourful and vibrant market stall, Antigua.

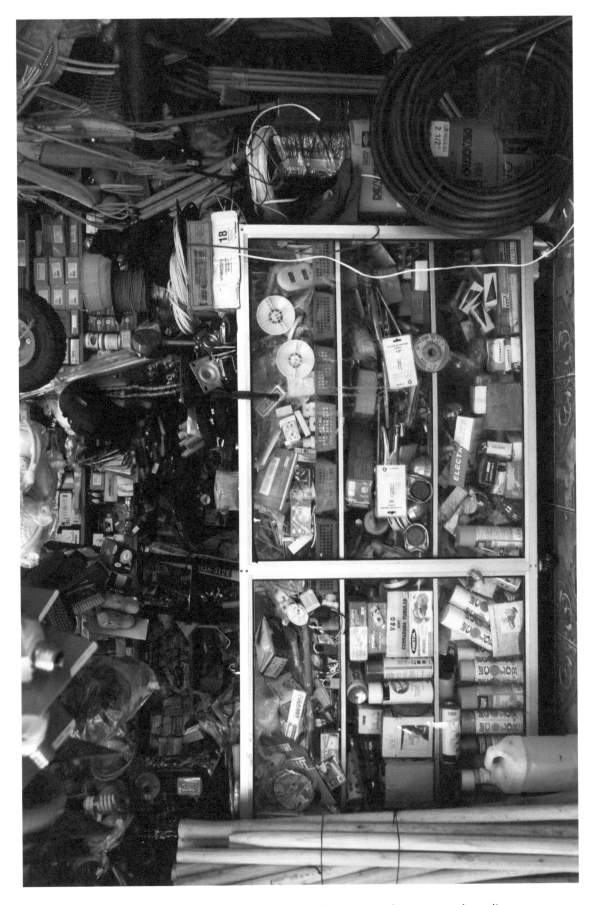

The 'general' stall, certainly the one with the biggest product range – by a distance.

One of the butchers at the municipal market.

Pancake preparation in the marketplace.

I was just taken by the different colour shades on this fruit stall.

The intriguingly named 'Horse Balls' fruit.

Church of San Jose el Viejo, Antigua.

Taking a different angle on the Church.

Welcome and come on in for a haircut to Barbarie Willie's in Antigua.

'Don't mind if I do, but careful with the cut-throat razor!'

Catedral de San Jose, Antigua.

The knowledgeable guide who found us at the Catedral ruins.

All that's left of the roof of Cathedral Church of St John after the 1974 earthquake.

The hollow shell of Cathedral Church of St John after the 1974 earthquake.

Street band of many ages – love the concentration on the face of the lad with the maracas.

One of many unusual items on sale at the Nim Po't crafts museum.

Well disguised lad watching life on Avenida Norte.

Announcing an event outside Le Merced church.

Smartly dressed band performing at the festival in front of Le Merced church.

Elaborate hair preparation that turned the heads of many a passer-by.

Colourful front to this vidrieria (glassware) shop.

Back-breaking work for this over-burdened local.

Typical cobblestone street near the municipal market, the first time I've seen tuk-tuks outside Asia.

Starting the climb up Pacaya Volcano.

Incredibly smooth slopes of the three volcanoes in view from the slopes of Pacaya.

Black lava landscape on the upper slopes of Pacaya.

Capitalising on the available natural energy from the volcano.

The almost bizarre site of a dead tree just over the next ridge.

Riding along a narrow ridge almost as far up Pacaya as the guide will take us.

Sulphur steam coming off the lava flow.

Taken with a zoom lens from the roof of the Cafe Sky in downtown Antigua.

No matter where you are in Guatemala amazing colours seem to be everywhere.

Looking down towards Panajachel on Lake Atitlan from the steep main road into town.

Local kids in Santa Catarina happy to let my daughter and I take their photos.

Youngster in parental arms at the restaurant next to Villa Santa Catarina.

Early morning view of Lake Atitlan from Santa Catarina.

First water taxi of the day picks up its passengers.

Early morning lake colours – I was drawn to the curved line of birds in the right foreground.

The main road through the centre of Santa Catarina.

Panajachel waterfront departure point for the ferry across Lake Atitlan.

En route across the Lake.

Outside the Alegre pub in San Pedro La Leguna, Lake Atitlan.

Youngster deep in concentration in a San Pedro La Leguna street.

The official stance on drugs.

After some gentle negotiation this lady was happy to have her photo taken.

Butcher hard at work in the market at San Pedro La Leguna.

Friendly face happy to have her picture taken whilst busy preparing pancakes.

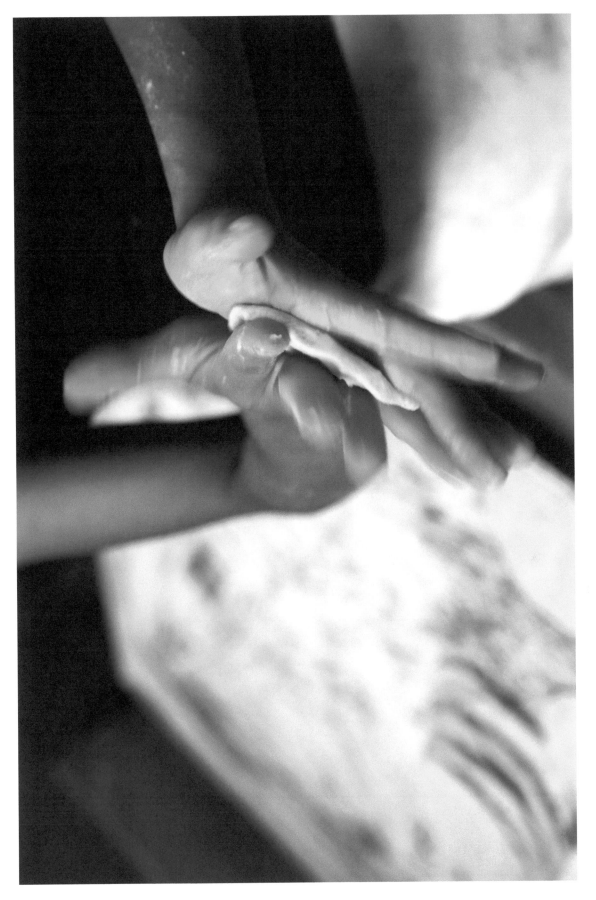

Pancake making – it's all in the hand action.

Rising lake levels at San Juan La Leguna, Lake Atitlan or the results of previous mudslides?

The drying affect of the warm sunshine at San Juan La Leguna.

It's a serious business this property watch! San Juan La Leguna.

Bizarre wall art on a San Juan La Leguna street.

Blue and green – who said they should never be together?

Fabulous expression, suspect she has a few stories to tell, and what of the cowboy in the background?

Sinister looking souvenir on sale at a gift shop in Santiago, Lake Atitlan.

Wonderfully laid back and relaxed looking gentleman watching life go by.

Colourful Santiago street scene.

Seemingly permanent walkway to bypass the affect on previous flooding on the Santiago waterfront.

The speedy way back from the Atitlan Hotel to Santa Catarina.

Spider monkey in the Reserva Natural, Panajachel, Lake Atitlan.

Atitlan Butterfly Sanctuary in the Reserva Natural, Panajachel.

Looking down to Santa Catarina from the road to Panajachel.

Late afternoon light on Lake Atitlan shot from Santa Catarina.

Young girls eager to sell an array of trinkets to visitors, and yes they managed it!

Multi-tasking weaver able to balance selling and child care.

Colourful display of weaved products on the roadside in Santa Catarina.

Weaver resplendent in her 'huipile' (blouse), the most important part of a Mayan ladies' costume.

The same weaver back to work.

Owner of the corner shop at the end of the road in which we were staying. Love the hat!

Aftermath of the 2010 mudslides in Panajachel.

Market traders on the steps of Santo Tomas Church, Chichicastenango.

One of the main ways through the Cichicastenango market.

Flower trader on the steps of Santo Tomas Church.

El Calveiro Church at the opposite end of the Chichicastenango market to the Santo Tomas Church.

Colourful and cute-looking hand-made childrens footwear.

Owner of the footwear stall.

Neighbouring and equally colourful market stall.

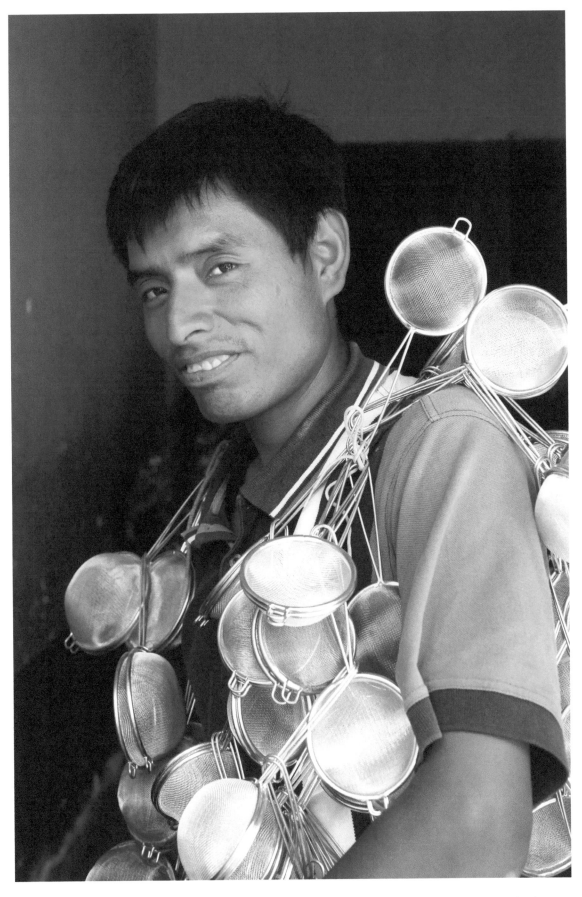

Mobile sieve salesman entering the market- a friendly face happy to be photographed.

Looking down onto the inside fruit and vegetable market.

Hive of activity in the fruit and vegetable market.

Carefully selecting their chosen tomatoes.

Watching the market, just liked the light on the side of his face.

One of many locals that appear as soon as you stop on the roadside.

Like the way the lad is looking straight down the camera lens, in contrast to the others.

Multi-coloured toucan in the forests at the Tikal ruins near Flores.

Daytime view from the top of Temple 4 at Tikal.

Climbing to the top of Temple 2 of these incredibly impressive Mayan ruins.

Grand Plaza shot from the top of Temple 2.

One small part of these extensive ruins at Tikal.

One of many coatimundi that are seen all over the ruins.

Temple 2 shot from the north acropolis.

Part of the northern acropolis.

The front of the 7 Temples Plaza.

The nuns arrive at the Tikal ruins.

Armed security guards are present for added safety.

Looking up to the tall Ceiba tree, the national tree of Guatemala.

First light across the rain forests shot from the top of Temple 4.

Watching the sun rise, hearing the jungle awaken - one of the most impressive sights and sounds I've ever encountered.

Just the temple tops left showing and within a few minutes the mist was gone as the sun rose.

Early light over the grand acropolis and Temple 1 shot from the top of Temple 2.

Also from Keith Hern

Available in Paperback, Amazon Kindle,

iBooks for the iPad, Kobo Books and many more formats.

www.mxpublishing.com

Source UK Ltd.
nes UK
88180220
003B/95